for GCSE

Practice for book I1 part B

PATHFINDER EDITION

Contents

PUBLISHED BY THE PRESS SYNDICATE OF THE UNIVERSITY OF CAMBRIDGE
The Pitt Building, Trumpington Street, Cambridge, United Kingdom

CAMBRIDGE UNIVERSITY PRESS
The Edinburgh Building, Cambridge CB2 2RU, UK
40 West 20th Street, New York, NY 10011-4211, USA
10 Stamford Road, Oakleigh, VIC 3166, Australia
Ruiz de Alarcón 13, 28014 Madrid, Spain
Dock House, The Waterfront, Cape Town 8001, South Africa

http://www.cambridge.org

First published 2001

Printed in Italy by Rotolito Lombarda
Typeface Minion   *System* QuarkXPress®

A catalogue record for this book is available from the British Library

ISBN 0 521 01252 X paperback

Typesetting and technical illustrations by The School Mathematics Project

17 Sequences

Sections A and B

1 Write down
   (a) the 5th square number
   (b) the 7th square number
   (c) the 10th square number
   (d) the 20th square number

2 From this grid of numbers write down
   (a) all the multiples of 8
   (b) all the square numbers
   (c) all the triangle numbers

28	29	30	31	32	33
34	35	36	37	38	39
40	41	42	43	44	45
46	47	48	49	50	51

3 Copy each of these sequences and find the next two terms
   (a) 6, 10, 14, 18, 22, … , …
   (b) 3, 6, 12, 24, … , …
   (c) 3, 8, 13, 18, 23, … , …
   (d) 10, 8, 6, 4, 2, … , …

4 Which of the sequences in question 3 are linear?

5 A sequence of numbers begins 2, 3, 5, 8, 12, 17
   (a) What are the next two terms?
   (b) Describe a rule to go from one term to the next.
   (c) Is the sequence linear?

6 A sequence of numbers begins 36, 20, 12, 8, …
   The rule for this sequence is 'add 4 to the last term then half it'.
   (a) What are the next three terms? Show all your working.
   (b) Is the sequence linear?

7 A sequences of numbers beings $^-3$, $^-5$, $^-9$, …
   The rule for this sequence is 'double the last term then add 1'.
   (a) What are the next three terms in the sequence?
   (b) Another sequence with the same rule starts $^-\frac{7}{8}$, $^-\frac{3}{4}$, $^-\frac{1}{2}$, … , …
       What are the next three terms?

8 Copy each of these sequences and fill in the missing numbers.

   These are cube numbers
   (a) 1, 8, … , 64, 125, …
   (b) 16, 8, 4, 2, 1, … , … ,
   (c) 81, 27, 9, 3, … , $\frac{1}{3}$ … , $\frac{1}{27}$
   (d) 1, 1, 2, 3, 5, … 13, 21, … , … ,

   These are called Fibonacci numbers

3

Section C

1 The nth term of a sequence is $2n + 5$. Write down
   (a) the first five terms of the sequence   (b) the 10th term   (c) the 100th term

2 The nth term of a sequence is $3n - 2$. Write down
   (a) the first five terms of the sequence   (b) the 20th term

3 A sequence begins $7, 5, 3, 1, ^-1, \ldots$
   (a) Which of these is its nth term? | $2n + 5$ | | $^-2n + 5$ | | $^-2n + 9$ |
   (b) Write down its tenth term.

4 The nth term of a sequence is $3 - 2w$. Write down
   (a) the first five terms of the sequence   (b) the 10th term

5 The nth term of a sequence is $30 - 3n$. Write down
   (a) the first five terms of the sequence   (b) the tenth term

6 The nth terms of six different sequences are:

   | $n + 2$ | | $2n$ | | n^2 | | $\frac{1}{2}n$ | | $2n + 1$ | | n |

   (a) Calculate the first five terms of each sequence.
   (b) Which of these sequences are linear?

Section D

1 A sequence begins $3, 7, 11, 15, 19, 23$

   Lucia says the nth term is 4n + 1   *Yasmina says the nth term is 4n – 1*

   Who is correct? What is the nth term of the sequence?

2 For each of the following sequences
   - find the next two terms
   - find the tenth term
   - find the nth term

   (a) $6, 10, 14, 18, 22, \ldots$ (b) $11, 21, 31, 41, 51, \ldots$
   (c) $1, 4, 7, 10, 13, \ldots$ (d) $5, 8, 11, 14, 17, \ldots$

3 A sequence begins $2, 5, 8, 11, 14, \ldots$
   (a) What is the 10th term?
   (b) Sam says the nth term of this sequence is $n + 3$.
       Explain why Sam is wrong and what is the nth term
       of this sequence?

   It goes up in 3's so it's n + 3

4 Here are five expressions for nth terms:

$5n$ $n + 1$ $n - 5$ $5n + 1$ $^-5n + 1$

Match each sequence below to its nth term above.

6, 11, 16, 21, 26 ... $^-4, ^-9, ^-14, ^-19, ^-24, ...$ $^-4, ^-3, ^-2, ^-1, 0, ...$

6, 7, 8, 9, 10 ...   5, 10, 15, 20, 25 ...

5 A sequence begins 3, 1, $^-1$, $^-3$, $^-5$, ...

(a) What are the next two terms?   (b) What is the nth term?

6 For each of the following sequences find the nth term.

(a) 8, 11, 14, 17, 20, 23, ...   (b) $^-3, ^-6, ^-9, ^-12, ^-15, ...$

(c) 2, $^-1$, $^-4$, $^-7$, $^-10$ ...   (d) 17, 14, 11, 8, 5, ...

Section E

1 The nth term of a sequence is $n^2 + 5$.

(a) Write down the first six terms of the sequence.

(b) Calculate the 10th term.

2 The nth term of a sequence is $2n^2 + 3$.

(a) Write down the first five terms of the sequence.

(b) Calculate the 10th term.

3 **A** 11, 14, 19, 26, 35, ...   **B** 2, 7, 12, 17, 22, ...   **C** 0, 3, 8, 15, 24, ...

(a) Which of these sequences is a linear sequence?

(b) What is the next term in each sequence?

(c) Find the nth term of each sequence.

Section F

1 A fencing design is modelled first with matchsticks.

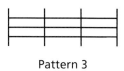

Pattern 1   Pattern 2   Pattern 3
5 sticks   9 sticks   13 sticks

(a) Sketch Pattern 4. How many sticks are in pattern 4?

(b) How many sticks are in Pattern 5?

(c) How many sticks are in Pattern 10?

(d) How many sticks are in the nth pattern?

2 A pattern is made with sticks.

Pattern 1
8 sticks

Pattern 2
15 sticks

Pattern 3
22 sticks

(a) How many sticks in Pattern 4?
(b) How many sticks in Pattern 5?
(c) Is the number of sticks a linear sequence?
(d) How many sticks in the nth pattern?
(e) Could I make one of these patterns with 48 sticks?
Give an explanation.

3 A5 booklets are made from folding and stapling A4 sheets of paper.

A4   fold   A5

An A5 booklet made from 2 sheets of A4 would have 8 pages and the centre pages would be numbered 4 and 5. Copy and complete this table:

Number of A4 sheets	1	2	3	4	10	n
Number of A5 pages in booklet	4	8	...	...	...	...
Page numbers on the centre spread	2 and 3	4 and 5	...	...	...	...

4 Jigsaw puzzles have:

corner pieces   edge pieces   and   middle pieces

(a) In this square jigsaw of size 5 by 5

(i) How many corner pieces are there?
(ii) How many edge pieces there?
(iii) How many middle pieces there?

(b) Copy and complete this table for different sizes of square jigsaw

Size of square jigsaw	4 by 4	5 by 5	6 by 6	10 by 10	n by n
Number of corner pieces	4				
Number of edge pieces					
Number of middle pieces					

Section G

1 'Pearlystrings' make necklaces and pendants from tiny pearls strung on nylon thread. These are some of their designs.
  For each design

  - draw Pattern 4

  - find out how many pearls are used in Pattern 5 and Pattern 10

  - find a rule for the number of pearls in Pattern n

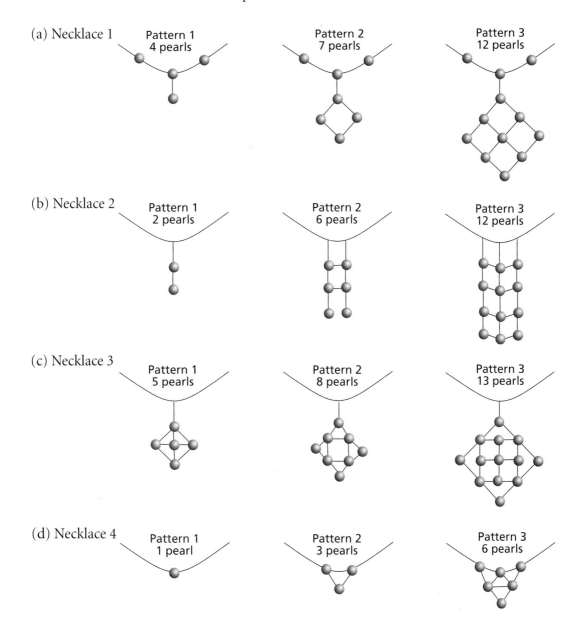

(a) Necklace 1

Pattern 1
4 pearls

Pattern 2
7 pearls

Pattern 3
12 pearls

(b) Necklace 2

Pattern 1
2 pearls

Pattern 2
6 pearls

Pattern 3
12 pearls

(c) Necklace 3

Pattern 1
5 pearls

Pattern 2
8 pearls

Pattern 3
13 pearls

(d) Necklace 4

Pattern 1
1 pearl

Pattern 2
3 pearls

Pattern 3
6 pearls

18 Percentage

Section A

1 Which is the best sale offer?

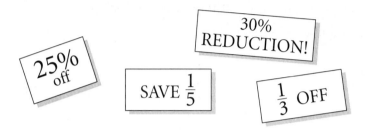

25% off

30% REDUCTION!

SAVE $\frac{1}{5}$

$\frac{1}{3}$ OFF

2 Write these fractions as percentages.

    (a) $\frac{3}{10}$ (b) $\frac{7}{20}$ (c) $\frac{9}{25}$ (d) $\frac{13}{50}$ (e) $\frac{2}{5}$

3 Write these percentages as fractions, simplifying where possible.

    (a) 45%   (b) 6%   (c) 17%   (d) 88%   (e) 80%

4 Write these fractions as decimals.

    (a) $\frac{3}{5}$ (b) $\frac{43}{50}$ (c) $\frac{9}{25}$ (d) $\frac{9}{20}$ (e) $\frac{7}{10}$

5 Write these decimals as fractions, simplifying where possible.

    (a) 0.37   (b) 0.55   (c) 0.06   (d) 0.8   (e) 0.95

6 Find pairs of matching percentages and decimals.

    A   0.37   B   1.6%   C 16%   D   30%   E   0.03

    F   0.16   G   37%   H 0.3   I   0.016   J   3%

7 Which of these pairs of statements are equivalent?

    (a) 20% of the passengers on the train had season tickets.
           $\frac{4}{5}$ of the passengers on the train did not have season tickets.

    (b) $\frac{5}{20}$ of the children were late for school.
           80% of the children arrived on time for school.

8 Write these fractions as percentages.

    (a) $\frac{84}{200}$ (b) $\frac{8}{40}$ (c) $\frac{8}{80}$ (d) $\frac{21}{30}$ (e) $\frac{3}{4}$

Section B

1 Work out
   (a) 50% of £36 (b) 25% of 60p (c) 10% of £8.20 (d) 5% of £80
   (e) 75% of £48 (f) 20% of £6 (g) 40% of £12 (h) 80% of £9

2 Richard went out for the day with £20 spending money.
   He spent 30% of his money on his train ticket.

   How much was the train ticket?

3 5% of the aeroplanes taking off from the local airport fly to the USA.
   If 160 aeroplanes leave the airport in one morning, how many of them fly to the USA?

4 There were 36 passengers on the bus.
   25% of the passengers got off the bus at the shopping centre.

   How many passengers were left on the bus?

5 On one Sunday, 40% of the 80 yachts moored in a marina were raced in a regatta.

   How many yachts were raced?

6 James and Javad went on holiday.
   James spent 80% of his £150 spending money and
   Javad spent 75% of his £180 spending money.

   Who spent most money and by how much?

7 Sarah backpacked around Europe on a 20 day trip.
   Unfortunately it rained on 35% of the days.

   How many days were rain free?

8 Work out $33\frac{1}{3}$% of
   (a) £15 (b) 36 kg (c) 24 km (d) 45 cm (e) 360 ml

9 Find $17\frac{1}{2}$% of
   (a) £200 (b) £48 (c) £160 (d) £2500 (e) £6.40

10 Find
   (a) 1% of £8 (b) 7% of £7 (c) 14% of £12 (d) 98% of £15 (e) 95% of £35

Section C

1 Write the following as percentages.

   (a) 48 out of 60   (b) 19 out of 25   (c) 210 out of 300   (d) 15 out of 20

2 On 3 mathematics assessments, Chloe scored

   (i)   (ii)   (iii)

      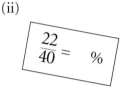   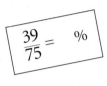

   (a) For each test, convert the marks to a percentage.

   (b) Which was her best result?

3 28 out of the 80 pages in a magazine were used for advertisements.

   What percentage of the magazine was used for advertisements?

4 Francis bought a bag containing 12 oranges.
   Unfortunately 3 of the oranges were rotten and could not be eaten.

   What percentage of the bag of oranges were edible?

5 Ashleigh did a survey of the 160 trees in her local park.
   She counted: 24 oak trees, 40 beech trees and the rest were chestnut trees.

   Calculate the percentage of each type of tree in the park.

6 Nootash decided to catalogue her CD collection.
   She found that she had 60 CDs altogether.

   (a) 9 of the collection had been given to her as presents.

   (b) 24 CDs were recorded by girl singers.

Section D

1 There are 280 pupils in year 7 in a school.

   (a) 40% of them travel to school by car.
        How many is this?

   (b) 42 pupils travel to school by bus.
        What percentage is this?

   (c) 55% of the pupils in the year are boys.
        How many girls are there in year 7?

2 A bag contains 120 counters of 2 different sizes coloured red, blue or yellow.

   (a) 15% of the counters are red.

   (b) Two fifths of the counters are blue.

      (i) What percentage is this?

      (ii) How many of the counters are blue?

   (c) 54 of the counters are yellow.

   (d) 75% of the counters are small.

3 320 scouts attended a Jamboree held.

   (a) 35% came from abroad.

   (b) 128 of the scouts took part in an orienteering challenge.

Section E

1 Work out:

   (a) 24% of 78   (b) 43% of 79   (c) 67% of 450

   (d) 17% of 5400   (e) 7% of 35.6   (f) 83% of 8750

2 Work out the following giving your answers to the nearest £1

   (a) 27% of £345   (b) 63% of £8935   (c) 34% of £725

3 The ingredients for a packet of 6 chocolate biscuits include
27% wheat flour and 11% milk chocolate.
A packet of the biscuits weighs 125 g.

   (a) What is the weight of wheat flour used in the biscuits?

   (b) What is the weight of milk chocolate on each biscuit?

4 Change these percentages into decimals.

   (a) 2.5%   (b) 13.9%   (c) 17.5%   (d) 0.8%

5 Work out the following giving your answers to the nearest penny:

   (a) 17.5% of £97   (b) 17.5% of £9.58   (c) 5.75% of £63.50

   (d) 0.75% of £95.65   (e) 18.6% of £125   (f) 7.25% of £34.45

6 Each year, Harry has to pay interest of 7.25% on a house loan of £42 000.
How much interest does he pay each year?

7 Gerald pays a garage a deposit of 37.5% for a car costing £6499.
How much deposit does he pay? (Give your answer to the nearest £1)

8 Martin bought a computer game for £34.99 using the Internet.
He was charged an extra £2.99 postage and packing.

(a) How much did the game cost including the postage and packing?

Martin was also charged VAT at 17.5% on the total cost of the game and the postage and packing.

(b) How much was the VAT?

(c) What was the total cost Martin had to pay for the game?

Section F

1 Work out

(a) 65 as a percentage of 97

(b) 1062 as a percentage of 3580

(c) 23.5 as a percentage of 37.6

2 37 marks were allotted to a science test.
Change the following marks achieved by students to percentages,
giving your answers to the nearest whole number.

(a) 26   (b) 31   (c) 8   (d) 19

3 284 students took a mathematics examination and 168 achieved a pass grade.

(a) What was the percentage of students who passed the examination?

(b) What percentage failed the examination?

4 The table shows the results of a survey of the reliabilty of cars.

(a) Calculate the percentage of each type of car in the sample that broke down.

(b) Which make was the most reliable?

(c) How many cars were there in the sample?

(d) What percentage of all the cars broke down?

Table showing number of breakdowns of cars up to 6 years in one year		
Make	sample size	breakdowns
A	1245	456
B	655	245
C	1456	312
D	890	180
E	386	125

5 In a test of batteries, 78 out of a sample of 126 'EVERLASTING' batteries ran for 18 hours whereas 65 out of a sample of 108 'GOODLIFE' batteries ran for 18 hours.

(a) What percentage of each set of batteries lasted for over 18 hours?

(b) What percentage of all the batteries lasted for more than 18 hours?

Section G

1 The table shows the percentage of the votes cast in an election received by the four candidates.

Candidate	Percentage
James Barrow	33.1
Martin Morris	22.4
Margaret Tyler	2.7
Susan Frinton	41.8

38 076 people voted in the election.

How many votes were received by each candidate?

2 A car manufacturer reduced the cost of a £13 599 car by £1 500.

Work out £1 500 as a percentage of £13 599.

3 In a survey of 681 'PHOTOIT' cameras, 6.9% had needed a repair.

(a) What percentage of the cameras had been trouble free?

(b) How many cameras had been trouble free?
   In a similar survey of 483 'PICFIX' cameras, 445 had been trouble free.

(c) What percentage of these cameras were trouble free?

4 (a) Between 1981 and 1985 there was an average of 20.3 million vehicles on the roads in the UK.
   During this time the average number of reported accidents each year was 249 000.
   In 1997 the number of vehicles had increased to 27 million and the number of accidents had fallen to 240 000.
   Calculate the number of accidents per year as a percentage of the number of vehicles on the road for

   (i) the period from 1981 to 1985 and   (ii) 1997

(b) In 1997, 1.1% of the 327 500 people who received injuries in traffic accidents, died of their injuries.
   How many people died in 1997 as a consequence of a traffic accident?
   Give your answer correct to the nearest hundred.

19 Graphs

Section A

1 Some of these equations will give you a graph which is a straight line.
Write down all the straight line graphs from this list.

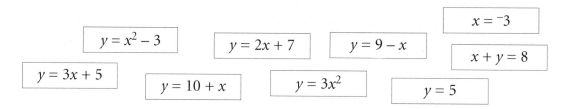

$x = {}^-3$

$y = x^2 - 3$

$y = 2x + 7$

$y = 9 - x$

$x + y = 8$

$y = 3x + 5$

$y = 10 + x$

$y = 3x^2$

$y = 5$

2 (a) Copy and complete this table of
values for the equation $y = 2$.

(b) Use the table to draw the graph of $y = 2$.

(c) Is the point (2, 5) on your line?

(d) Is the point (3, 2) on your line?

x	$^-2$	$^-1$	0	1	2	3	4
y	2				2		

3 The diagram shows the graphs of the
equations $y = 1$, $x = 1$, $y = {}^-3$ and $x = {}^-3$.

(a) Copy the diagram carefully and label
each of the four lines.

(b) Write down the coordinates of the point
where the line $x = 1$ crosses the line $y = {}^-3$.

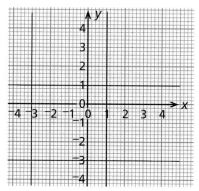

4 (a) Explain how you can find out whether the point (3, 2)
is on the line whose equation is $2x + 3y = 12$.

(b) Find the value of y on this line when $x = 6$.

(c) Find the value of y on this line when $x = 0$.

(d) Draw the graph using axes marked from 0 to 6 for both x and y.

(e) Use your graph to find the value of y when $x = 5$.

(f) Use your graph to find the value of x when $y = 3$.

Section B

1 *Lend-a-hand* is a company offering to help with any job.
   They charge a £5 starting fee and then £6 per hour.

   (a) What is the total cost for help for 2 hours?

   (b) How much would it cost for help for 4 hours?

   (c) Copy and complete the table for the costs for different times.

time (hours)	0	1	2	3	4	5	6	7	8
Cost (£)	5	11							

   (d) Draw a graph showing how the cost varies.
        Use axes with time (t) across from 0 to 8 hours and cost (c) up the page
        from £0 to £60.

   (e) Plot the points from your table and join them.
        Label the graph '*Lend-a-hand*'.

   (f) Use your graph to estimate the total cost for a time of $3\frac{1}{2}$ hours.

2 *We're cheaper* is a rival company.
   They have no starting fee, but charge an hourly cost of £7.

   (a) What is the cost of 2 hours help with *We're cheaper*?

   (b) Calculate the cost of 6 hours help.

   (c) Copy and complete this table for *We're cheaper*.

time	0	1	2	3	4	5	6	7	8
cost				21					

   (d) On the same axes that you used for question 1,
        plot the points from your table, join them, and label the graph *We're cheaper*.

   (e) Find the number of hours which would cost the same with either company.

Section C

1 Two of the following points are on the graph of $y = x^2 - 5$.
   Work out which two points are on the graph and write them down.
   $(0, 3)$ $(1, {}^-4)$ $(4, 8)$ $(5, 0)$ $(0, 5)$ $(0, {}^-5)$ $({}^-2, {}^-9)$

2 (a) Copy and complete this table of values for $y = x^2 + 2$.

x	${}^-3$	${}^-2$	${}^-1$	0	1	2	3
x^2		4			1		9
$x^2 + 2$		6			3		11

   (b) On graph paper, draw axes with x from ${}^-3$ to 3 and y from 0 to 12.
        Plot the points from your table and join them up with a curve.

   (c) Use your graph to estimate the value of y when $x = 1.5$.

   (d) At what values of x does the graph have the value 7 (give your answers to 1 d.p.).

   (e) Use your graph to solve the equation $x^2 + 2 = 6$.

3 (a) Copy and complete this table of values for the graph $y = 3x^2 - 4$.

x	$^-3$	$^-2$	$^-1$	0	1	2	3
x^2	9	4			1		9
$3x^2$	27	12			3		
$3x^2 - 4$	23	8			$^-1$		

(b) Draw axes with x from $^-3$ to 3 and y from $^-5$ to 25.
Draw the graph of $y = 3x^2 - 4$.

(c) Use your graph to solve the equation $3x^2 - 4 = 15$.

(d) What is the least value that y can take?

4 Draw the graph of $y = x^2 - 4x + 3$ for values of x between 0 and 4.

(a) Draw the graph's line of symmetry on your graph.

(b) Find the minimum value of y.

Section D

1 At Northgate Sports Centre there are three paddling pools of different shapes for children. Paul Northage's job is to fill the pools using a hose-pipe, from which the water flows in at a steady rate.

These are sketches of the three pools.

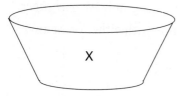 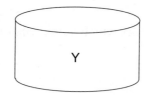 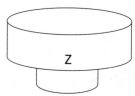

(a) Which description of filling the pools with water goes with which pool?

   R: The water level rises steadily for the whole time.

   S: The water level goes up quite quickly at first, then changes and goes up more slowly.

   T: The water level starts by going up quite quickly but gets gradually slower and slower.

(b) Which graph goes with which pool?

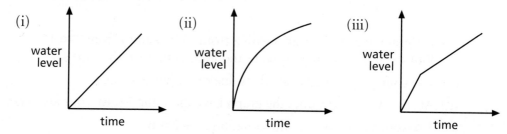

2 This graph shows the number of people in Northgate Sports Centre during one particular day.

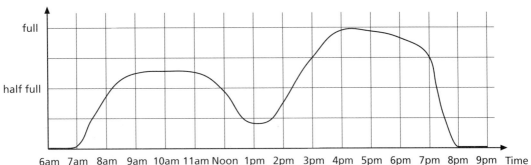

(a) What time do you think the Sports Centre opened?

(b) When do you think that the Sports Centre closed?

(c) When were there most poeple at the centre?

(d) Paul likes the Centre to be more than three-quarters full. For how many hours during the day was the centre more than three-quarters full?

3 Look at these graphs. Three of the graphs describe situations from the Sports Centre.

(a) Match the graphs to the correct descriptions.

(b) Suggest a situation for the spare graph.

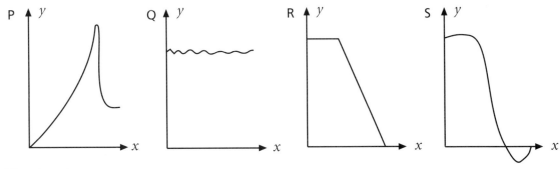

The situations:

    A: The height (y) above the water of someone diving from the highest diving board, against time (x).

    B: The speed (y) of a swimmer riding down a water chute, against time (x).

    C: The temperature (y) in the sauna, against time (x).

20 *Using a calculator*

Sections A, B and C

1 Do these calculations, giving each answer to 3 significant figures.

   (a) $6.84 + 0.72 \times 1.95$ (b) $(3.84 - 1.92) \times 1.67$ (c) $20.8 - 15.6 \times 0.85$

2 Here is a calculator sequence.

    $\boxed{4}\boxed{2}\;\boxed{\times}\;\boxed{3}\boxed{5}\;\boxed{-}\;\boxed{2}\boxed{3}\;\boxed{\div}\;\boxed{1}\boxed{6}\;\boxed{=}$

Which of these calculations does it do?

   A $42 \times \dfrac{35 - 23}{16}$ **B** $\dfrac{42 \times 35 - 23}{16}$ **C** $\dfrac{42 \times (35 - 23)}{16}$

   D $42 \times 35 - \dfrac{23}{16}$ **E** $42 \times \left(35 - \dfrac{23}{16}\right)$

3 Give the results of these calculations to 2 decimal places.

   (a) $\dfrac{14.7 - 9.6}{2.8}$ (b) $3.47 + \dfrac{11.62}{0.59}$ (c) $\dfrac{12.31 - 4.76}{5.84 + 1.37}$

   (d) $\dfrac{18.70}{9.42 - 1.48}$ (e) $\dfrac{20.5 \times 1.4}{15.7 - 10.9}$ (f) $\dfrac{16.5}{0.83 \times 0.46}$

Sections D and E

1 (a) Without using a calculator, work out a rough estimate for

$$\frac{48.7 \times 0.38}{22.4 - 9.6}$$

   (b) Do the calculation above on your calculator,
       giving the result to 3 significant figures.

2 For each calculation below,

   (i)   work out a rough estimate without using a calculator

   (ii)   calculate the result to 3 significant figures

   (a) $\dfrac{88.7 \times 0.58}{11.2}$ (b) $\dfrac{624 \times 0.284}{31.7 - 9.8}$ (c) $\dfrac{621}{41.5 \times 28.8}$

3 Do these calculations, giving the result correct to 3 significant figures.

   (a) $\dfrac{\sqrt{58.2 - 11.7}}{5.3}$ (b) $\dfrac{12.7}{(6.2 - 1.8)^2}$ (c) $\dfrac{9.3 + \sqrt{12.5}}{9.3 - \sqrt{12.5}}$

   (d) $\sqrt{\dfrac{13.6}{12.9 - 5.8}}$ (e) $\dfrac{73.2}{\sqrt{(6.8 + 5.4)}}$ (f) $3.75 + \dfrac{6.47}{\sqrt{2.48}}$

Mixed questions 4

1 120 students applied to go on a summer sports camp.
Only 65% of those who applied went on the sports camp.
How many students went on the camp?

2 Calculate each of these, giving the result to 2 decimal places.

(a) $\dfrac{7.69 - 2.92}{2.8}$ (b) $\dfrac{3.04}{4.22 \times 0.85}$ (c) $\sqrt{19.6 \times 4.2^2}$

(d) $3.22 - (2.81 - \sqrt{11.4})$ (e) $(6.7 - 9.8)^2$ (f) $\sqrt{3.3^2 + 0.8^2 - 1.8^2}$

3 The nth term of a certain sequence is given by the expression $n^2 + 5$.
  (a) What is the first term of the sequence?
  (b) Work out the seventh term of the sequence.
  (c) One of the terms has the value 174. Which term is it?

4 Carla fires a plastic 'rocket' straight up in the air from a toy launcher.
The rocket's height, h metres, is given by this formula.

$$h = 27t - 5t^2$$

t is the time in seconds from when Carla fires the rocket.

  (a) Copy and complete this table.

t	0	1	2	3	4	5	6
$27t$	0	27					
$5t^2$	0	5					
$h = 27t - 5t^2$	0	22					

  (b) On suitable axes, draw the graph of $h = 27t - 5t^2$.
  (c) From the graph, what is the greatest height reached by the rocket?
  (d) At what value of t does it reach this height?
  (e) When does the rocket hit the ground?
  (f) What percentage of the rocket's time in the air is it
      25 metres or more above the ground?

21 Unitary method

Section A

1 3 dining room chairs cost £150.
   How much would 6 chairs cost?

2 Here are the ingredients to make spinach
   and mushroom omelette.

   (a) How much spinach is needed for
       6 people?

   (b) How much soured cream is needed for
       4 people?

   (c) How much butter is needed for
       3 people?

3 The cost of 3 breakfast bars is 90p.
   What is the cost of 5 bars?

4 4 blank videos cost £6.
   What is the cost of 7 videos?

5 2 batteries cost £2.70.
   What would be the cost of 6 batteries?

6 3 loaves of wholemeal bread cost £2.07 altogether.
   How much would I pay for 5 loaves of wholemeal bread?

7 4 tins of beans weigh 860 g altogether.
   What would be the weight of 3 tins of beans?

8 A stack of 5 books is 7.5 cm high.
   What would be the height of a stack of 8 of these books?

Spinach and Mushroom Omelette

Serves 2

• 200 g spinach
• 40 g butter
• 125 g mushrooms
• 10 ml mustard
• 140 ml soured cream
• nutmeg and seasoning

Sections B and C

1 For each calculation, simplify by cancelling common factors and then evaluate it.

   (a) $\dfrac{17 \times 10}{2}$ (b) $\dfrac{13 \times 18}{6}$ (c) $\dfrac{21}{4} \times 12$ (d) $15 \times \dfrac{27}{5}$

2 For each calculation, simplify by cancelling common factors and then evaluate it.

   (a) $\dfrac{24 \times 33}{88}$ (b) $\dfrac{18}{42} \times 49$ (c) $\dfrac{45 \times 16}{40}$ (d) $35 \times \dfrac{27}{21}$

3 Mrs White buys 6 boxes of chocolate, each containing 20 chocolates, to share equally between the children in her tutor group.
There are 24 children in Mrs White's tutor group.

How many chocolates do they each receive?

4 6 table tennis balls weigh 15 g.

What is the weight of 20 table tennis balls?

5 10 small sugar lumps weigh 18 g.

What is the weight of 25 sugar lumps?

6 12 identical coins weigh 150 g.
A pile of these coins weighs 250 g.

How many coins are there in the pile?

7 Jane's hair grows 12 mm in 30 days.

   (a) If it continued to grow at the same rate, how long will it grow in 40 days?

When Jane had her hair trimmed, the hairdresser snipped off 18 mm of hair.

   (b) How long will it take for her hair to grow back to its original length?

8 28 litres of water were collected from a dripping tap in 21 minutes.

If the water continued to drip at the same rate, how much water could be collected in 30 minutes?

Section D

1   Fingernails grow 0.05 cm in 7 days.
    How long do finger nails grow in a year?
    Give your answer correct to the nearest 0.01cm.

2   Mr Jones travelled 182 miles on 23.6 litres of petrol.
    The petrol tank in his car holds 55 litres.

    How many miles would Mr Jones expect to travel on a full tank of petrol?

3   Martin used 16.4 litres of petrol to drive 130 miles.

    How much petrol would he expect to need for a journey of 250 miles?

4   A piece of metal weighing 193 grams has a volume of $25\,cm^3$.

    (a) What is the weight, to the nearest gram, of a similar piece of metal which has a
         volume of $38\,cm^3$?

    Another piece of the same metal weighs 124 g.

    (b) What is the volume of this piece of metal?

    Give your answer correct to the nearest cm^3.

5   The table shows the amount of carbohydrate and fat in 100 g of different
    chocolate bars.

	Carbohydrate	Fat
100 g of Soft Centre	61.3 g	24.3 g
100 g of Chocolate Crisp	55.9 g	30.1 g

    A Soft Centre bar weighs 16.7 g and a Chocolate Crisp weighs 21.9 g.

    (a) Calculate the amount of carbohydrate in a Soft Centre bar.
         Give your answer correct to the nearest 0.1g.

    (b) Which chocolate bar contains the most fat and by how much?
         Give your answer correct to the nearest 0.1 g.

Section E

1 When driving on the continent, Anne drove between 2 towns which were 325 km apart. The mileage recorder in her car showed that the distance travelled was 202 miles. She then drove a further 178 km.

(a) Convert 178 km into miles and work out how many miles she travelled altogether.

On the next day, she drove 246 miles

(b) How many kilometres is this?

2 Hayley bought some CDs from America on the internet. She was charged $39.99. Hayley could have bought the same CDs in her local music store for £28.98. The exchange rate was £1 = $1.41.

(a) Which was the cheapest method of buying the CDs?

(b) How much cheaper was it?

3 Mohammed travelled from the USA to Japan as part of a worldwide business trip. When he arrived in Japan he converted 350 dollars ($) into Japanese Yen (¥). The exchange rate was $1 = ¥118

(a) How many Yen did he receive in exchange for his $350?

He saw a mobile phone in a shop selling for ¥4500

(b) What would be the price of the phone in dollars?

4 Jean-Paul travelled from Paris to New York. On arrival at the airport he exchanged his Euro (€) travellers cheques for dollars ($). He exchanged €50 for $46.

(a) How many Euros would he have needed to exchange to receive $200?

Jean-Paul took a total of €840 to New York.

(b) How many dollars could he receive for this amount?

5 A certain set of scales measure in pounds (lbs) and kilogrammes. A 14 lb bag is put on the scales and the scales show that it weighs 6.356 kg.

(a) What would be the weight in kilogrammes of a 20 lb bag?

A small boy weighs 42 kg.

(b) What would be his weight in pounds?

22 *Similarity*

Sections B and C

1 Measure the length of all the sides of the original and scaled copy of this shape.

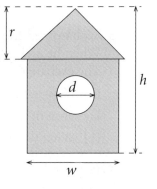

Copy

Original

What is the scale factor used to make the copy?

2 Rammi and Alex both drew a scale plan of the same bird box. They made a table to show the lengths on their plans.

Copy and complete this table.

	Rammi's plan	× ?	Alex's plan
Height of box (h)	9.6 cm		14.4 cm
Width of box (w)	6.8 cm		
Diameter of hole			4.8 cm
Height of roof (r)	4.2 cm		

3 Measure the two shortest sides on each of these right-angled triangles.

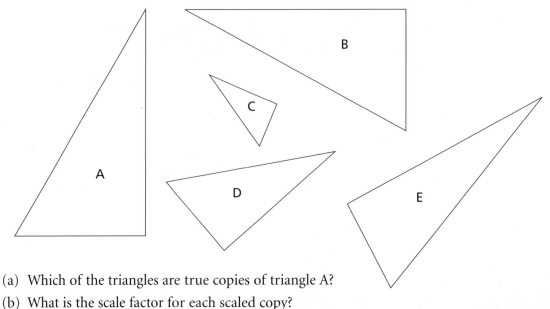

(a) Which of the triangles are true copies of triangle A?

(b) What is the scale factor for each scaled copy?

Section D

1 These triangles are all similar. (They are not drawn to scale).

For each triangle:

  (i) find the scale factor from the shaded triangle

  (ii) the length of the missing side.

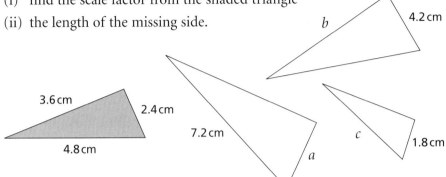

2 These triangles are all similar.

Find the missing angles.

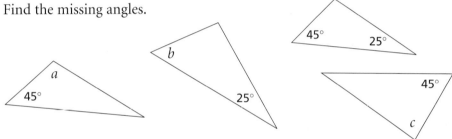

3 These two triangles are similar.

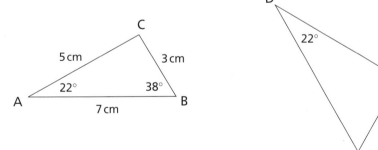

  (a) Find angle DEF.

  (b) Calculate the length of the side DE.

Section E

1 For each of these rectangles find the ratio $\dfrac{\text{longest side}}{\text{shortest side}}$.
Use this to find pairs which are true copies of each other.

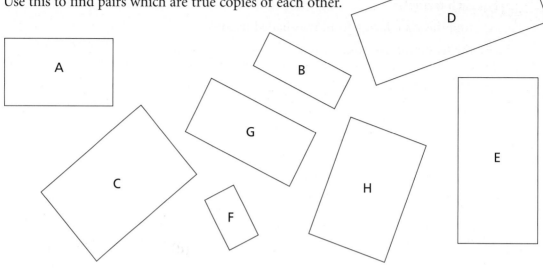

2 The table below shows the
height (h) and width (w)
of some true copies of this rectangle.

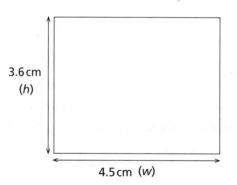

3.6 cm
(h)

4.5 cm (w)

(a) Calculate the ratio $\dfrac{\text{width}}{\text{height}}$.

(b) Copy and complete the table.

Height (h)	Ratio	Width (w)
5.80 cm		
12.60 cm		
		7.6 cm

3 Copy and complete this table for a set of scaled copies.

Height (h)	Ratio	Width (w)
30 cm		24 cm
		4.2 cm
7 cm		

23 Fractions

Section A

1 Work out

   (a) $\frac{3}{8}$ of 40   (b) $\frac{3}{5}$ of 40   (c) $\frac{5}{6}$ of 9   (d) $\frac{7}{8}$ of 72

2 Write in its simplest form   (a) $\frac{20}{36}$ (b) $\frac{25}{45}$ (c) $\frac{18}{60}$

Sections B and C

1 Mary's cat eats $\frac{2}{3}$ of a tin of cat food each day.
How many tins does it eat in 14 days?

2 Work out

   (a) $\frac{3}{4} \times 5$ (b) $\frac{3}{5} \times 7$ (c) $\frac{4}{5} \times 9$ (d) $10 \times \frac{3}{4}$ (e) $14 \times \frac{2}{5}$

3 Work out

   (a) $\frac{1}{5}$ of 14   (b) $\frac{3}{8}$ of 20   (c) $\frac{5}{6}$ of 8   (d) $\frac{2}{3}$ of 11

Sections D, E and F

1 Work out

   (a) $\frac{1}{3} \div 4$ (b) $\frac{1}{4} \div 5$ (c) $\frac{1}{3} \div 9$ (d) $\frac{1}{2} \div 6$ (e) $\frac{1}{5} \div 5$

2 Work out

   (a) $\frac{2}{3} \div 6$ (b) $\frac{3}{4} \div 4$ (c) $\frac{3}{5} \div 2$ (d) $\frac{5}{8} \div 3$ (e) $\frac{5}{6} \div 3$

3 Work out

   (a) $\frac{1}{3}$ of $\frac{1}{8}$ (b) $\frac{1}{3}$ of $\frac{5}{8}$ (c) $\frac{3}{4} \times \frac{5}{8}$ (d) $\frac{2}{3} \times \frac{3}{8}$ (e) $\frac{3}{10} \times \frac{4}{5}$

4 Work out   (a) $\frac{1}{3} \times 1\frac{1}{2}$ (b) $\frac{1}{2} \times 1\frac{1}{3}$ (c) $1\frac{1}{2} \times 1\frac{1}{3}$

Section G

1 Work out

   (a) $\frac{1}{2} + \frac{1}{5}$ (b) $\frac{1}{2} - \frac{1}{5}$ (c) $\frac{1}{2} \times \frac{1}{5}$ (d) $1\frac{1}{2} - \frac{1}{5}$

2 Work out

   (a) $\frac{3}{8} + \frac{1}{3}$ (b) $\frac{3}{8} \times \frac{1}{3}$ (c) $\frac{3}{8} - \frac{1}{3}$ (d) $2\frac{3}{8} - 1\frac{1}{3}$

3 Work out   (a) $\frac{1}{3}$ of $13\frac{1}{2}$ (b) $\frac{2}{3}$ of $13\frac{1}{2}$

24 Speed, distance, time

Section A

1. Calculate the average speed of each of the following.
   State the units of your answers.

   (a) A car that goes 117 miles in 3 hours.

   (b) A man who walks 9 km in $1\frac{1}{2}$ hours.

   (c) A bus that travels 38 miles in 2 hours.

   (d) A dog that runs 200 m in 40 seconds.

2. A plane flying at constant speed travels 450 km in $1\frac{1}{2}$ hours.

   (a) How far would it fly in 3 hours?

   (b) What is the speed of the plane in km/h?

3. Ken recorded his mileometer readings during a journey.

Start	Break	End
32403	32518	32677

   (a) Ken drove for $2\frac{1}{2}$ hours before his break. What was his average speed?

   (b) He drove for 3 hours after his break. What was his average speed after his break?

   (c) What was his average driving speed for the whole journey?

Section B

1. Describe each of these journeys fully.

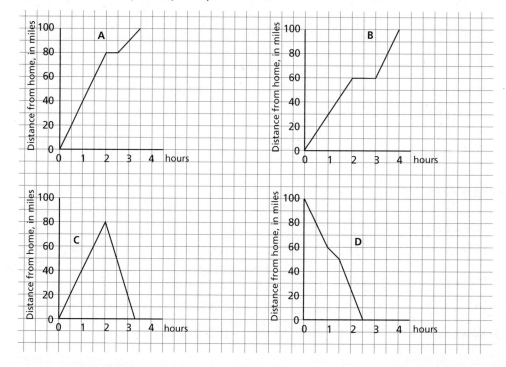

28

2 Randeep drives from Birmingham to Liverpool. Barry does the same journey by coach. This graph shows their journeys.

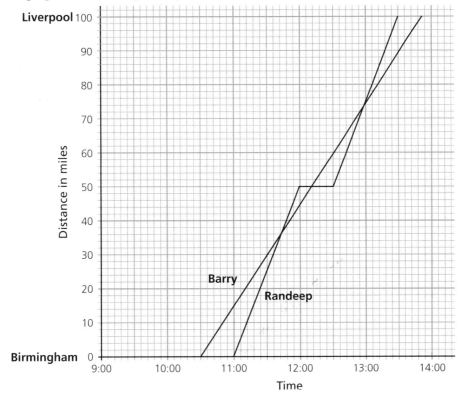

(a) How far is it from Birmingham to Liverpool?

(b) At what time did Barry leave Birmingham?

(c) How long did it take him to travel to Liverpool?

(d) At what speed did he travel to Liverpool?

(e) Randeep stopped on the way. For how long did he stop?

(f) At what time did Randeep first overtake Barry?

(g) How far apart were they at 12:30?

(h) At what speed did Randeep drive after his break?

(i) How much later than Randeep did Barry arrive at Liverpool?

3 Make a copy of the axes above on graph paper.

(a) Sasha leaves Liverpool at 10:00 and drives towards Birmingham at 40 m.p.h. Draw and label the graph of her journey.

(b) Lee leaves Birmingham at 11:30 and drives towards Liverpool at 60 m.p.h., for $1\frac{1}{2}$ hours. He stops for half an hour, and then drives the rest of the way to Liverpool at 40 m.p.h.. Draw and label the graph of his journey.

(c) At what time do Sasha and Lee pass each other?

(d) How far are they from Birmingham when they pass?

Section C

1 Sue cycles at 32 km/h for 2 hours. How far does she travel?

2 A hot air balloon takes off at 7:30 and lands at 9:00. It travels at 4 m.p.h. How far does it travel in this time?

3 An ostrich can run at a speed of 18 m/s. How far does it travel in

    (a) 10 seconds   (b) 30 seconds   (c) 1 minute   (d) 5 minutes.

4 A helicopter flies at 320 km/h for 30 minutes. How far does it travel?

5 Dave drives for $2\frac{1}{2}$ hours at an average speed of 52 m.p.h.. His mileometer reads 13584 at the start of his journey.

    What is his mileometer reading at the end of the journey?

Sections D and E

1 A bus travels 5 miles in 20 minutes. Calculate its average speed in miles per hour.

2 Fraser walks $\frac{1}{2}$ mile in 10 minutes. Calculate his speed in miles per hour.

3 A boat travels at 24 km/h. How far does it travel in

    (a) 30 minutes   (b) 20 minutes   (c) 5 minutes.

4 A car travels a distance of 37 miles in 50 minutes.

    (a) Change 50 minutes into decimals of an hour.

    (b) Calculate the average speed of the car in m.p.h.

5 Sam walks a distance of 10 km in 1 hour 25 minutes. Calculate her average speed in km/h, to 1 decimal place.

6 A plane is flying at a speed of 260 m.p.h. How far does it go in 55 minutes?

Section F

1 A dolphin swims at a steady speed of 30 km/h. How long does it take to swim 75 km?

2 A train travels at a speed of 80 m.p.h. How long does it take to travel 40 miles?

3 An antelope can run at a speed of 26 m/s. How long does it take to run 1 km?

4 A plane flies at a steady speed of 280 m.p.h.
   How long, in hours and minutes, does it take to travel 644 miles?

5 Kate drives at an average speed of 52 m.p.h. Her journey is 120 miles.
   If she leaves home at 9:30, at what time does she arrive?

Section G

1 Calculate the missing entries in this table.

Distance	Time	Average Speed
45 miles	(a)	50 m.p.h.
(b)	2 hours 30 minutes	48 km/h
200 m	25 seconds	(c)
120 miles	(d)	45 m.p.h.
(e)	1 hour 20 minutes	39 km/h

2 Maurice Greene broke the world 100 m sprint record on 16 June 1999.
   His time was 9.79 seconds.

   Calculate his speed in m/s, to 1 decimal place.

3 The moon moves around the earth at an average speed of 3700 km/h.

   How far does it travel in 1 day?

4 In Japan, the Bullet train can travel at an average speed of 206 km/h.
   It takes $2\frac{1}{2}$ hours to travel from Tokyo to Osaka.

   Calculate the distance from Tokyo to Osaka.

5 During the first Zeppelin trial in July 1900, it flew 6 km in 17 minutes.

   Calculate the speed of the Zeppelin in km/h to 1 decimal place.

Mixed questions 5

1 Work these out

   (a) $\frac{1}{8} \times 32$ (b) $45 \times \frac{1}{9}$ (c) $\frac{5}{6} \times 36$ (d) $92 \times \frac{1}{4}$ (e) $\frac{3}{4} \times 19$

   (f) $28 \times \frac{1}{3}$ (g) $\frac{1}{10} \div 4$ (h) $\frac{4}{5} \div 3$ (i) $\frac{5}{6} \times \frac{3}{10}$ (j) $\frac{1}{4} + \frac{2}{3}$

2 What scale factors are used here to copy

   (a) shape Q to shape S

   (b) shape P to shape Q

   (c) shape P to shape S

   (d) shape P to shape R

   (e) shape S to shape P

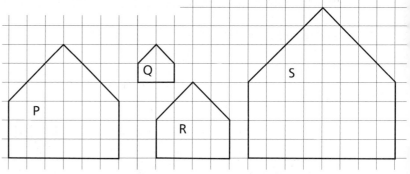

3 This is part of a label on some cheese in a supermarket.
What would 500 g of this cheese cost?

Weight	Price
246 g	£1.51

4 17 identical marbles weigh 141 g.
How much would 11 of the same marbles weigh, to the nearest gram?

5 A painter takes an hour and a quarter to paint one door.
How many doors can he paint in an $7\frac{1}{2}$-hour day?

6 Tom saw this book on sale at an airport.
He had some pounds and some euros in his pocket.
He had obtained his euros at the rate of 1.55 euros to each pound.

Which is the cheaper way for him to pay – with pounds or with euros?

7 A plane travels for $4\frac{3}{4}$ hours at 392 m.p.h.
How far does it go?

8 A designer has a photograph 134 mm wide by 206 mm high.
She wants to reduce it so its width is 98 mm to fit in a
column of a magazine.

   (a) What scale factor should she use?

   (b) How high will the picture be when it is printed in the magazine?

25 Constructions

Do all this work on plain paper

Sections A and B

1 Follow this a method for constructing a line
through a point P parallel to another line AB.

(a) Draw a straight line AB.

(b) Mark point P on one side of the line.

(c) Mark another point Q on the same side of the line.

(d) Construct the perpendicular line RS from Q to AB.

(e) Construct the perpendicular from P to RS.

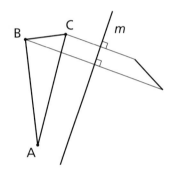

2 (a) Draw a line *m* at an angle and draw
a triangle ABC on one side of the line.

(b) Construct perpendiculars from the
points A, B and C to the line *m*.

(c) Construct the reflection of the
triangle in the line *m*.

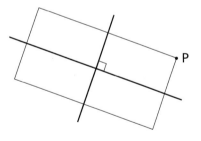

3 (a) Construct two lines at right angles.

(b) Mark a point not on the lines.

(c) Construct the rectangle formed
by reflecting the point in both lines.

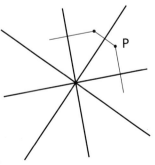

4 (a) Construct four lines crossing at 45°.

(b) Mark a point between two of the lines
about 5 cm from where the lines cross.

(c) Construct the octagon formed by repeatedly
reflecting the point in the lines.

Sections C and D

1 (a) Construct a right-angled triangle.

   (b) Construct the perpendicular bisectors of the 3 sides.

   (c) What is special about the point where they meet?

   (d) Using this point as a centre, draw the circle passing through the three vertices of the triangle.

2 (a) Draw a quadrilateral like the one labelled A.

   (b) Find the midpoints of the sides by constructing their perpendicular bisectors.

   (c) Join the 4 midpoints to make a new quadrilateral.

   (d) What is special about this new quadrilateral?

   (e) Do you get the same result for a quadrilateral like B?

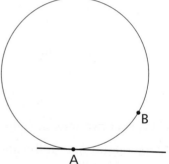

3 (a) Draw a line about 8 cm long and mark on it a point A.

   (b) Mark a point B about 3 cm from the line.

   (c) Construct the circle which passes through B and touches the line at A (the line is a tangent to the circle).

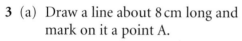

4 (a) Draw a triangle ABC with sides between 8 cm and 16 cm long.

   (b) Find the midpoint of each side of the triangle by constructing the perpendicular bisectors. The line going from the mid point of a side to the opposite corner is called a median of the triangle.

   (c) Draw the three medians AD, BE and CF – they should pass through a single point P.

   (d) Measure the lengths of AP, PD, BP, PE, CP and PA.

   (e) Calculate the ratios

     (i) AP:PD   (ii) BP:PE   (iii) CP:PF

   (f) What do you notice about your answers?

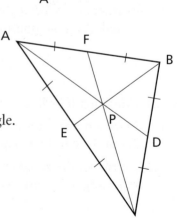

26 Gradient

Section A

1 Find the gradient of
   each line in the diagram.

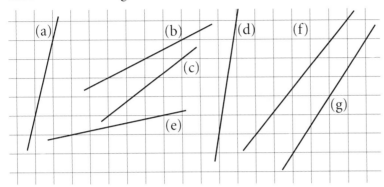

2 Find the gradient of the line joining the points with coordinates $(2, 3)$ and $(7, 7)$

3 Kyle is planning a walk up Walton Hill.
   He draws a sketch of the hill.

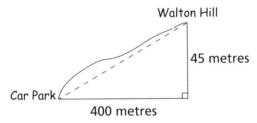

Find the average gradient of the hill, correct to 3 decimal places.

4 In Wengen, Switzerland the cable car takes you up to the nearest peak.
   The cable car starts at a height of 1300 m above sea level.
   The peak is at a height of 2229 m above sea level.

   According to the map, the horizontal distance covered is 1280 m.

   (a) What height does the cable car climb?

   (b) What is the average gradient of the climb as a decimal?

Section B

1 What rates of flow are shown by the following graphs?

(a) 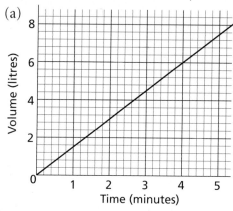 (b)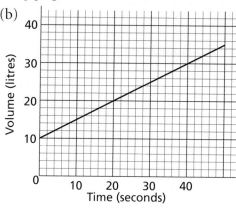

2 (a) For the graphs below, work out the gradient of each line.

(b) What does each gradient represent?

(i) 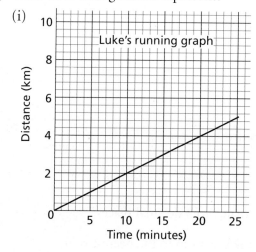 (ii)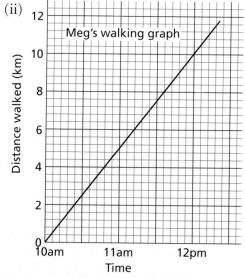

3 (a) Work out the gradient of this line, correct to 1 d.p.

(b) What does the gradient represent?

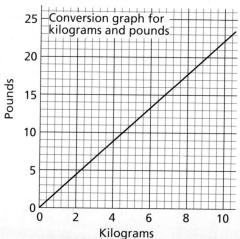

Section C

1 Find the gradient of each line in the diagram below.

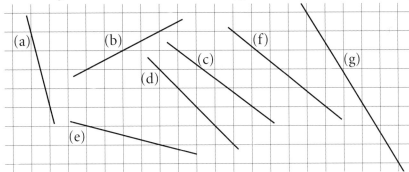

2 This graph shows the variation in temperature experienced as a mountaineer climbs up a mountain.

(a) Calculate the gradient of the line.

(b) What does the gradient represent?

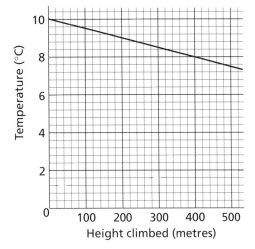

3 Find the gradient of the line joining the points with coordinates (1, 3) and (6, 1).

4 This graph shows the volume of water in a bath.

(a) Find the gradient of each straight line segment A, B, C and D.

(b) What do you think happened at

   (i) 4 minutes from the start

   (ii) 6 minutes from the start

   (iii) 16 minutes from the start.

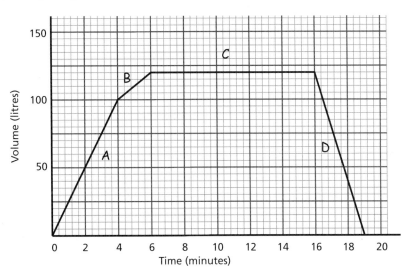

27 *Indices*

Sections A and B

Pattern 1   Pattern 2   Pattern 3

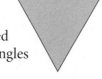 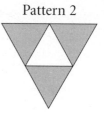 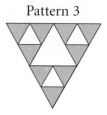

1 The diagram shows the first 3 patterns in a series.

To make a new pattern, every shaded triangle is cut up into 3 shaded triangles and a white triangle.

How many shaded triangles will there be in pattern
  (a) 4   (b) 5   (c) n

2 Match each expression with an answer from the box.

81	5	32
125	2	16
1	27	

  (a) 5^0 (b) 5^3 (c) 2^1 (d) 4^2

  (e) 3^3 (f) 5^1 (g) 2^5 (h) 3^4

3 Evaluate

  (a) $2^5 - 8$ (b) $3^2 + 3^3$ (c) $2^3 + 7^0$ (d) $3^4 \div 3^1$

  (e) $2^2 \times 5^2$ (f) $4^3 \div 2^4$ (g) $5^3 \div 3^0$ (h) $7^1 \times 1^7$

4 Work out the value of 2×3^n when

  (a) $n = 0$ (b) $n = 1$ (c) $n = 3$ (d) $n = 4$

5 For each of the following, work out the value of p.

  (a) $2^p = 32$ (b) $5^p = 125$ (c) $p^1 = 11$ (d) $p^2 = 81$

  (e) $5^p = 1$ (f) $10^p = 1000$ (g) $2^p = 2$ (h) $p^4 = 10\,000$

6 Work out the value of t in

  (a) $5^t + 5 = 30$ (b) $4^t \div 8 = 8$ (c) $5^2 - 4^t = 3^2$ (d) $5 \times 5^t = 625$

  (e) $10^2 \div t = 5^2$ (f) $2^t \times 5^3 = 1000$ (g) $2^5 + t^2 = 57$ (h) $t^t = 27$

7 Find the value of the following when $a = 2$.

  (a) $a^2 + a^3$ (b) $2a^3$ (c) $a^3 - a^2$ (d) a^5

  (e) $3a^4$ (f) $a^0 + a^1$ (g) $a^4 + a^4 + a^4$ (h) $a^2 \times a^3$

Sections C and D

1 Write the answers to these using indices.

  (a) $5^3 \times 5^4$ (b) $7^3 \times 7^8$ (c) $5^3 \times 5^8$ (d) $9^4 \times 9^5$

  (e) $2^3 \times 2^5 \times 2^7$ (f) $4 \times 4^7 \times 4^7$ (g) $8^0 \times 8 \times 8^2$ (h) $6^0 \times 6^2 \times 6^9$

2 $2^{10} = 1024$

Use this value to work out without a calculator

(a) 2^9 (b) 2^8 (c) 2^{11} (d) 2^{12}

3 The table shows some powers of 3.

3^4	3^5	3^6	3^7	3^8	3^9	3^{10}	3^{11}
81	243	729	2187	6561	19 683	59 049	177 147

Use the table to evaluate

(a) 81×243 (b) 81×2187 (c) 729×243 (d) 243^2

4 Match each expression with an answer from the box.

(a) $a \times a \times a$ (b) $a^3 \times a^2$ (c) $a^5 \times a^5$ (d) $a^3 \times a$

(e) $a^2 \times a^3 \times a^4$ (f) $a \times a^5 \times a$ (g) $a \times a^3 \times a^2$ (h) $a^4 \times a^4 \times a^4$

$$\boxed{\begin{array}{ccc} a^{10} & a^{12} & a^9 \\ a^3 & a^7 & a^5 \\ a^4 & a^6 & \end{array}}$$

5 Some powers of 5 are evaluated below.

$5^4 = 625$ $5^5 = 3125$ $5^6 = 15\ 625$ $5^7 = 78\ 125$ $5^8 = 390\ 625$ $5^9 = 1\ 953\ 125$

Use these to evaluate each of the following.

(a) $(5^2)^2$ (b) $(5^3)^2$ (c) $(5^2)^4$ (d) $(5^3)^3$

6 Simplify each of these.

(a) $(3^4)^2$ (b) $(2^5)^3$ (c) $(a^2)^3$ (d) $(b^1)^3$ (e) $(c^0)^2$

7 Simplify each of these.

(a) $2a \times 3a^3$ (b) $e^2 \times 5e^3$ (c) $3f \times 2f^3$ (d) $3h^5 \times 7h^3$

(e) $2d^4 \times 3d^5$ (f) $3g^2 \times 5g^6$ (g) $2p \times 3p^2 \times 4p^3$ (h) $3m \times 2m^7 \times m^3$

8 Copy and complete these multiplication walls.

(a)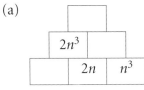

(b)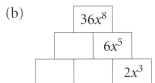

(c)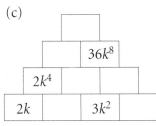

(d)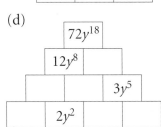

9 Simplify

(a) $(2c^2)^3$ (b) $(3k^0)^4$ (c) $(5b^4)^3$ (d) $(2v^3)^5$

Sections E, F and G

1 Write the answers to these using indices

(a) $5^8 \div 5^3$ (b) $4^7 \div 4^0$ (c) $6^3 \div 6$ (d) $3^5 \div 3^2$

(e) $\dfrac{2^7}{2^3}$ (f) $\dfrac{5^6}{5^0}$ (g) $\dfrac{4^5}{4}$ (h) $\dfrac{7^8}{7^7}$

2 Write the answers to these using indices.

(a) $\dfrac{3^5 \times 3^4}{3^2}$ (b) $\dfrac{5^3 \times 5^2}{5^4}$ (c) $\dfrac{(6^2)^3}{6^4}$ (d) $\dfrac{7^5 \times 7^2}{7^4 \times 7^3}$

3 Find the value of w in each of the following expressions.

(a) $7^5 \div 7^2 = 7^w$ (b) $\dfrac{4^6}{4^w} = 4$ (c) $\dfrac{3^w}{3^0} = 3^5$

(d) $\dfrac{a^7}{a^2} = a^w$ (e) $\dfrac{b^9}{b^w} = b^4$

4 Simplify each of these.

(a) $d^5 \div d^3$ (b) $\dfrac{e^7}{(e^3)^2}$ (c) $\dfrac{b^4 \times b^2}{b^3}$ (d) $\dfrac{s^3 \times s^4}{5^6 \times s}$ (e) $\dfrac{t^5 \times t^2}{t^2 \times t}$

5 This table shows some powers of 6.

6^2	6^3	6^4	6^5	6^6	6^7	6^8
36	216	1296	7776	46656	279936	1679616

Use the results in the table to evaluate these.

(a) $\dfrac{1296}{36}$ (b) $\dfrac{46656}{7776}$ (c) $\dfrac{279936}{1296}$

(d) $\dfrac{1679616}{46656}$ (e) $\dfrac{216 \times 7776}{279936}$ (f) $\dfrac{1296^2}{216}$

6 Simplify these.

(a) $\dfrac{7b^5}{b^2}$ (b) $\dfrac{9c^6}{3c}$ (c) $\dfrac{20n^4}{4n^2}$ (d) $\dfrac{16m^5}{2m^4}$ (e) $\dfrac{30s^8}{5s^4}$

7 Simplify by cancelling.

(a) $\dfrac{3^3}{3^5}$ (b) $\dfrac{2^5}{2^{10}}$ (c) $\dfrac{5}{5^6}$ (d) $\dfrac{4^3}{4^8}$

8 Simplify by cancelling

(a) $\dfrac{k^4}{k^8}$ (b) $\dfrac{m^3}{m^7}$ (c) $\dfrac{t^5}{t^6}$ (d) $\dfrac{s}{s^4}$

9 Simplify by cancelling

(a) $\dfrac{4a^3}{a^5}$ (b) $\dfrac{2c^7}{6c^2}$ (c) $\dfrac{15d^8}{10d^3}$ (d) $\dfrac{e}{3e^5}$

(e) $\dfrac{10k^3}{15k}$ (f) $\dfrac{18q^6}{15q^2}$ (g) $\dfrac{4r^3}{10r^8}$ (h) $\dfrac{9p}{12p^5}$

Section H

1 Find the missing numbers in each statement below

   (a) $2^{-3} = \dfrac{1}{\blacksquare}$ (b) $\dfrac{1}{2^4} = 2^{\blacksquare}$ (c) $4^{-2} = \dfrac{1}{4^{\square}}$ (d) $5^{\blacksquare} = 1$

2 Find the missing number in each statement below

   (a) $\frac{1}{8} = 2^{\blacksquare}$ (b) $\blacksquare^{-2} = \frac{1}{9}$ (c) $\frac{1}{5} = 5^{\blacksquare}$ (d) $4^{-2} = 1$

3 2^{-3} is equivalent to the fraction $\frac{1}{8}$

Write the following as fractions

   (a) 4^{-1} (b) 2^{-5} (c) 3^{-2} (d) 5^{-2} (e) 10^{-3}

4 $10^{-2} = \dfrac{1}{10^2} = \dfrac{1}{100} = 0.01$ as a decimal.

Write the following as decimals.

   (a) 10^{-1} (b) 10^{-3} (c) 5^{-2} (d) 2^{-3} (e) 100^{-1}

5 Find the missing expressions in the following

   (a) $x^{-2} = \dfrac{1}{\blacksquare}$ (b) $\dfrac{1}{\blacksquare} = z^{-4}$ (c) $w^{-1} = \dfrac{1}{\blacksquare}$

6 Put the following numbers in order of size, starting with the smallest.

   (a) 2^{-3} 10^{-1} $\frac{1}{9}$ $\frac{1}{5^2}$

   (b) 4^{-1} 3^{-2} $\frac{1}{2}$ $\frac{1}{2^3}$

Section I

1 Write the answers to these as a single power.

   (a) $4^4 \times 4^{-2}$ (b) $7^{-3} \times 7^5$ (c) $2^{-5} \times 2^3$ (d) $3^5 \times 3^{-5}$

   (e) $6^{-6} \times 6^3$ (f) $8^{-2} \times 8$ (g) $5^{-3} \times 5^{-2} \times 5$ (h) $2^5 \times 2^{-3} \times 2^{-2}$

2 Write the answers to these as a single power.

   (a) $4^3 \div 4^5$ (b) $\dfrac{3^2}{3^3}$ (c) $2 \div 2^4$ (d) $\dfrac{5}{5^3}$

   (e) $\dfrac{7^4}{7^5}$ (f) $9 \div 9^5$ (g) $\dfrac{6^4}{6^6}$ (h) $2^3 \div 2^9$

3 Match each of these with one of the answers in the box.

   (a) $s^4 \times s^{-3}$ (b) $s^{-2} \times s^4$ (c) $s \times s^{-6}$ (d) $s^{-3} \times s^{-4}$

   (e) $s^{-5} \times s^{-1}$ (f) $s \times s^{-1}$ (g) $s^2 \times s^{-3}$ (h) $s^{-1} \times s^{-1} \times s^{-1}$

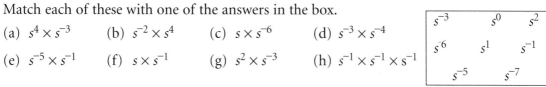

s^{-3} s^0 s^2 s^6 s^1 s^{-1} s^{-5} s^{-7}

4 Simplify each of these.

   (a) $k^2 \div k^5$ (b) k^4 (c) $k^2 \div k^7$ (d) k

   (e) k^5 (f) $k \div k^6$ (g) k^2 (h) $k^4 \div k^7$

5 Copy and complete these multiplication grids

(a)

X	s^{-2}	s^5	s^{-1}	
		s^6		
s^{-4}				
	s^3			
s^{-2}				s

(b)

X				
r^3				
		r^4		r^2
r^6	r^5	r^2	r^3	
r^2				

Section J

1 The diagram shows 3 'trees'.

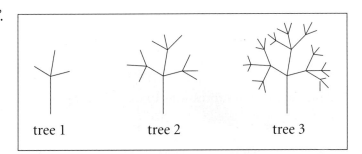

tree 1   tree 2   tree 3

To get to a new tree, 2 new 'branches' grow from every old 'branch'.
Tree 2 has 9 new branches.

How many branches will there be on

(a) tree 4   (b) tree 5   (c) tree n

2 Evaluate these.

(a) $4^2 + 5$ (b) $3^5 - 3^3$ (c) $2^{-1} + 4^{-1}$ (d) $3^2 - 2^{-1}$

(e) $3^4 \times 3^{-2}$ (f) $2^3 \div 4^0$ (g) $2^5 \times 4^{-2}$ (h) $6^2 \div 3^2$

3 Simplify each of these.

(a) $3g^3 \times 5g^{-1}$ (b) $\dfrac{16h^4}{4h^3}$ (c) $2k^{-3} \times 3k^{-3}$ (d) $\dfrac{20m^4}{5m^6}$

(e) $6p^{-2} \times 3p^2$ (f) $2q \times 3q^{-1} \times 5$ (g) $\dfrac{10y^3}{5y^{-1}}$ (h) $\dfrac{5z^{-2}}{z^{-4}}$

4 Find the value of n in the following

(a) $2^n = 64$ (b) $10^n = 0.01$ (c) $n \times 3^3 = 3^5$ (d) $\dfrac{4^2}{8 \times 4^n} = 8$

28 Pythagoras

Sections A and B

1 Work out the missing area or length in each of these.

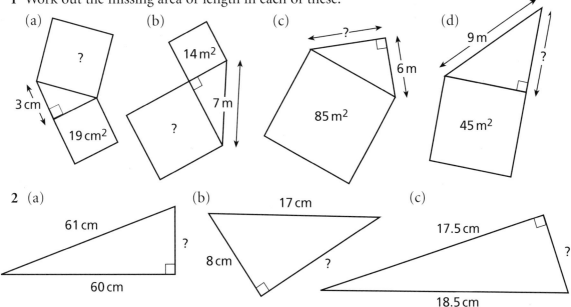

(a)

(b)

(c)

(d)

2 (a)

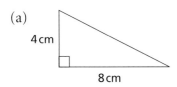

(b)

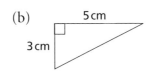

(c)

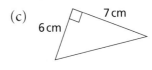

Section C

1 Calculate the longest side of each of these right-angled triangles.
   Give the length to 1 d.p.

(a)

4 cm

8 cm

(b)

5 cm

3 cm

(c)

6 cm

7 cm

2 Calculate the hypotenuse of a right-angled triangle whose other two sides are

   (a) 4 cm and 5 cm   (b) 9 cm and 13 cm

   (c) 7 cm and 7 cm   (d) 6 cm and 16 cm

3 Calculate the length of the side marked ? in each of these right-angled triangles.

(a)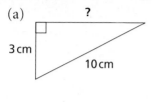

(b)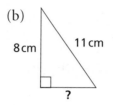

(c)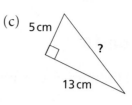

(d)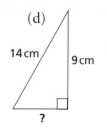

(e)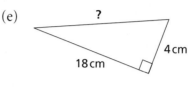

Section D

1 The two shorter sides of a set-square are both 7.4 cm long.
How long is the longest edge? (Give the answer to 1 d.p.)

2 A square has sides 4.5 cm long. How long is each diagonal?

3 The bottom end of a ladder is 3 m from the wall of a house.
The top end reaches 5 m up the wall.
Draw a sketch and calculate the length of the ladder.

4 An equilateral triangle can be split into
two identical (congruent) right-angled
triangles, as shown here.

(a) Use Pythagoras' theorem to calculate the
height h cm of an equilateral triangle
who sides are each 10 cm long.

(b) Calculate the area of the equilateral triangle.

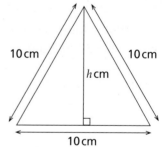

5 Sketch a grid and mark the points P ($^-$2, 1) and Q (5, 3).
Calculate the distance from P to Q, to 2 d.p.

6 Calculate to 2 d.p. the distance between (1, 0) and (6, $^-$2).

7 Calculate the distance between each of these pairs of points.

(a) (0, 2) and (6, 0)　　　　　　(b) (0, 2) and 4, $^-$1)

(c) ($^-$2, $^-$3) and (5, $^-$1)

29 *Looking at expressions*

Section A

1 Simplify the following by collecting like terms

(a) $p^2 + 3p + 2p^2 - 4p$ (b) $4x^2 + 3x - x^2 - 3$ (c) $7y + 5y^2 - 2 + 3y$

(d) $8n^2 - 5n - 3n^2 + 5$ (e) $5l + l^2 - 6 - 3l^2$ (f) $k^2 - 6k + 3k^2 + 10k + 1$

2 Find the value of each expression when $x = 3$

(a) $x^3 + x^2 + 7 - x^3$ (b) $x^2 + 3x - 2x$

(c) $6x^2 - 5x^2 + 2x + 2$ (d) $x^3 + x^2 + x - x^2 + 5$

3

| A | $m^2 + m^3$ | B | $2m - m^3$ | C | $4m^2 - 2m - 2$ | D | $2 - m^2$ |

(i) Find pairs of expressions that add to give

    (a) $m^3 + 2$ (b) $m^2 + 2m$ (c) $3m^2 - 2m$ (d) $4m^2 - m^3 - 2$

(ii) Find three of the expressions that add to give $2m + 2$.

Sections B and C

1 Multiply out the brackets from

(a) $x(x + 6)$ (b) $4(3a + 5)$ (c) $4a(2 - a)$

2 Find the missing expressions in these statements.

(a) $n(\blacksquare) = n^2 - 3n$ (b) $3x(\blacksquare) = 6x - 9x^2$

(c) $4p(\blacksquare) = 4p^2 - 8p^3$ (d) $2k(\blacksquare) = 6k + 2k^4$

3 Find three pairs of matching expressions

| A | $n(n^2 + 3)$ | B | $3n^2 + 3n^3$ | C | $n^3 + 3n$ | D | $n^3 + 3n^2$ | E | $3n(n + n^2)$ | F | $n^2(n + 3)$ |

4 Multiply out the brackets from

(a) $4k(3k - 2)$ (b) $3p(p^3 - p^2)$ (c) $4w^2(2 + 3w^2)$ (d) $x^3(4x^2 - x)$

5

| 4 | n | $3n$ | n^2 | $3n - 2$ | $n - 1$ |

Find pairs of the above expressions that multiply to give

(a) $n^2 - n$ (b) $4n^2$ (c) $3n^2 - 3n$ (d) $12n - 8$

(e) $9n^2 - 6n$ (f) $3n^3 - 2n^2$ (g) $n^3 - n^2$

6 Factorise each of these.

(a) $4x + 8$ (b) $a^2 - 3a$ (c) $3k^3 - 2k$ (d) $12g - g^2$ (e) $3y^2 - 6$

7 Find the missing expressions in these statements.

(a) $4p$ (■) $= 4p^2 + 12p$ (b) $9n$ (■) $= 18n^2 + 9n$

(c) $3x$ (■) $= 6x^3 + 9x$ (d) y^2 (■) $= 4y^4 + 3y^3$

8 Factorise each of these completely.

(a) $8x^2 + 10x$ (b) $3d^2 + 15d$ (c) $4y + 12y^2$ (d) $10h^2 - 25h^3$

9

A	C	D	E	I	L	N	O	S
4	3	x	$x - 2$	$x + 1$	$x - 1$	5	$x^2 + 3$	$5x$

Fully factorise each expression below as the product of two factors.
Use the code above to find a letter for each factor.
Rearrange the letters in each part to spell a person's name.

(a) $5x^2 + 15$, $4x + 4$, $5x^2 - 5x$

(b) $4x - 4$, $3x^2 + 9$, $5x + 5$

(c) $x^2 + x$, $5x - 5$, $4x - 8$

*10 (a) Factorise $5n + 10$

(b) Explain how the factorisation tells you that $5n + 10$ will be a multiple of 5 to any integer n.

Section D

1 Find the value of each expression when $x = 3$ and $y = 4$

(a) $2xy + y$ (b) $3y^2 - x$ (c) $2x^2 + y^2 - 2$ (d) $4x + 2y^2 - 3y$

(e) $(xy)^2$ (f) x^2y (g) xy^2 (h) x^2y^2

2 Find the value of each expression when $a = 2$, $b = 5$ and $c = 6$

(a) $2a + 3b + c$ (b) $ab + bc$ (c) $4ab - c^2$

(d) $ab^2 - 3c + b$ (e) $\dfrac{bc}{a}$

3 Simplify the following expressions by collecting like terms

(a) $3n + m + 4n - 3m$ (b) $mn + 3n^2 + 3mn + 2 + 6n^2$ (c) $8m - n^2 + 4m + 3n^2$

4

A $\boxed{a^2 - b}$ B $\boxed{2a + b}$ C $\boxed{4b - b^2}$ D $\boxed{2a^2 - b^2}$

Find pairs of the above expressions that add to give

(a) $3a^2 - b^2 - b$ (b) $a^2 + 2a$ (c) $2a + 5b - b^2$ (d) $2a^2 - 2b^2 + 4b$

5 Find the result of each multiplication in its simplest form.

(a) $a \times 3b$ (b) $2x \times 5y$ (c) $2k \times 3m$ (d) $4n \times 3p$ (e) $5x \times 4y$

6 Find the result of each multiplication in its simplest form.

(a) $3x^2 \times 4y$ 　　　　　(b) $4ab \times 3b^2$ 　　　　　(c) $2xy^2 \times 4x^2y^4$

7 Find the missing expression in each statement.

(a) $3x \times \square = 12xy$ 　　(b) $\square \times 6m^2n = 18m^3n^2$ 　　(c) $4p^2q \times \square = 20p^5q^4$

8 | $3x$ | $4y$ | $5xy$ | $4x^2$ | $3x^2y$ | x^3y |

Find pairs of the above expressions that multiply to give

(a) $4x^3y^2$ 　　　　　(b) $15x^3y^2$ 　　　　　(c) $12x^3$

(d) $16x^2y$ 　　　　　(e) $3x^5y^2$ 　　　　　(f $5x^4y^2$

9 Expand and simplify the following.

(a) $(4ab)^2$ 　　　　　(b) $(2mn)^3$ 　　　　　(c) $(4a^2b^3)^3$

10 Simplify each of these.

(a) $\dfrac{2xy}{x}$ 　　　　　(b) $\dfrac{12x^2y}{3xy}$ 　　　　　(c) $\dfrac{9x^2y^3}{3x^2y^2}$

11 Simplify each of these.

(a) $\dfrac{ab^2}{3b}$ 　　　　　(b) $\dfrac{4xy}{y^3}$ 　　　　　(c) $\dfrac{12k^2l^3m}{36k^3lm^2}$

12 Simplify each of these.

(a) $\dfrac{4ab \times 3a^2b}{6b}$ 　　　(b) $\dfrac{7mn^2 \times 3m^3n}{2mn^2}$ 　　　(c) $\dfrac{4a^2b^3 \times 2b^4}{3a^3b}$

Section E

1 Expand each of these.

(a) $4(3a + 2b)$ 　　(b) $b(4a - 5b)$ 　　(c) $5(2a + 3b)$ 　　(d) $b(5a - 3b)$

2 Factorise each of these.

(a) $5a - 5b$ 　　　(b) $4a + 12b$ 　　　(c) $6n - 15m$ 　　　(d) $xy + 2x$

(e) $n^2 - 5n$ 　　　(f) $ab + a^2$ 　　　(g) $3ab^2 - 7b$ 　　　(h) $4ab^2 - 6a^2b$

3 Expand each of these.

(a) $ab(3a - 2b)$ 　　　(b) $6x(y + 3x)$ 　　　(c) $3k^2(4l + 5)$

4 Factorise each of these completely.

(a) $5mn^2 - 15m^2n$ 　　(b) $x^2y + 3xy^3$ 　　(c) $6k^2l^2 - 4kl$

(d) $3ab^2 + 6ab^3$ 　　(e) $4p^2q^3 + 10pq^2$ 　　(f) $5x^2y + 10y^3$

5

A	C	E	I	L	N	O	P	R	S	Y
$4x$	3	$3x$	xy	$2x-y$	$xy-1$	$3y^2$	$3x+2y$	x^2y+2	$x+y$	$2x-5y$

Fully factorise each expression below as the product of two factors.
Use the code above to find a letter for each factor.
Rearrange each set of letters to spell an item found in a school bag.

(a) $3x^2y + 2xy^2$, $3x^2y - 3x$, $6x - 3y$

(b) $6xy^2 - 15y^3$, $3xy - 3$, $4x^3y + 8x$

(c) $4x^3y + 8x$, $3x^2 + 3xy$, $3x^3y + 6x$

6 Factorise each of these completely.

(a) $4x^2y^3 + 12x^4y^2$ (b) $16x^2y^3 - 4xy$ (c) $5x^4y + x^2y^3$ (d) $p^4q^5 - 3p^5q^3$

Section F

1 (a) Find a formula for the perimeter of each shape below.
Use P to stand for the perimeter each time.

(b) Find a formula for the area of each shape.
Use A to stand for the area each time.

(i)

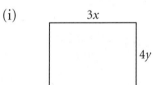

(ii)

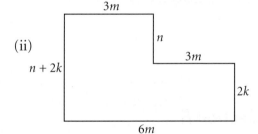

2 Find a formula for the volume of each prism.
Use V to stand for the volume each time.

(i)

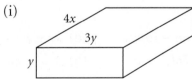

(ii)

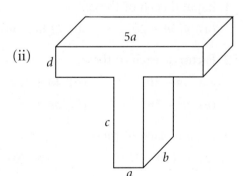

*3 (a) Find a formula for the volume of each prism.

(b) Find a formula for the surface area of each prism.

(i)

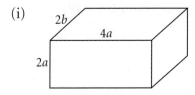

(ii)

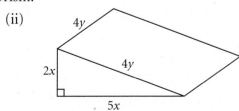

30 Triangles and polygons

Sections A, B and C

1 Draw sketches to show how an equilateral triangle
   can be split up into

   (a) two right-angled triangles

   (b) a trapezium and an equilateral triangle

   (c) a kite and two right-angled triangles

   (d) a parallelogram and two different-sized equilateral triangles

   (e) three kites

2 (a) What special kind of quadrilateral is shape ABCD?

   (b) Find the angles marked with letters.

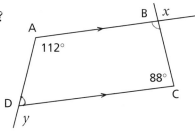

3 (a) What special kind of triangle is triangle PQR?

   (b) What special kind of triangle is triangle QRS?

   (c) Find the angles marked with letters.

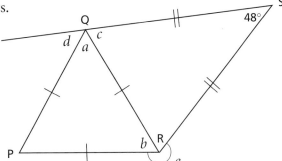

4 Find the angles marked with letters.

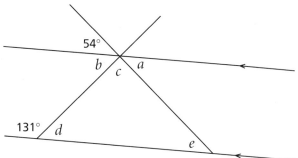

Sections D and E

1 Find the missing angles in each of these polygons.

(a)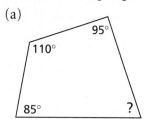

(b)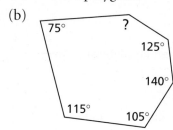

(c)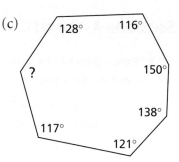

2 This is part of a regular polygon.
   The point P is the centre of the polygon.

(a) How many sides does the whole polygon have?

(b) Find the marked angles.

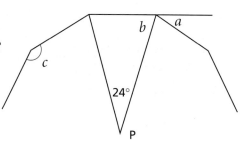

3 This pattern is made from six regular pentagons, all the same size.

(a) What special type of quadrilateral is the shaded shape in the middle?

(b) Calculate the four angles of the shaded quadrilateral.

4 This is a regular pentagon with two diagonals drawn in. Calculate the angles marked with letters.

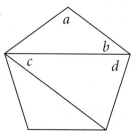

5 Calculate the missing angle.

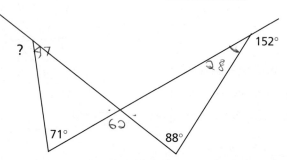

31 Gradients and equations

Sections A and B

1 For each of these lines:

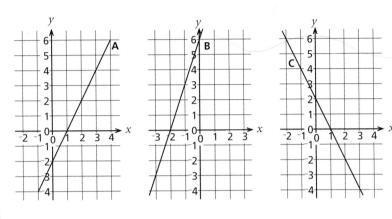

(a) find the gradient

(b) find the y-intercept

(c) write down the equation of the line.

2 (a) Plot the points $(1, 9)$ and $(^-2, ^-3)$ on suitable axes.

(b) Join the points and find the equation of the line.

3 (a) Plot the points $(2, 1)$ and $(^-4, 7)$ on suitable axes.

(b) Join the points and find the equation of the line.

4 Write down the equation of the line

(a) with gradient 5 that crosses the y-axis at $(0, ^-3)$.

(b) with gradient $^-10$ and y-intercept 4

5 For each of these lines:

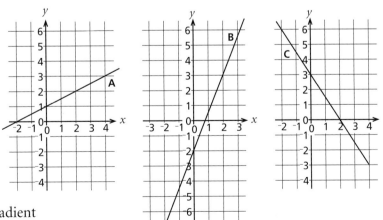

(a) find the gradient

(b) find the y-intercept

(c) write down the equation of the line.

6 Find the equation of each of these lines.

(a)

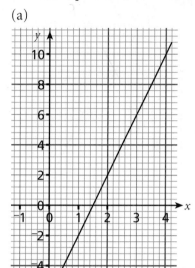

(b)

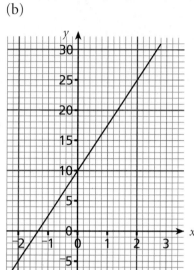

(c)

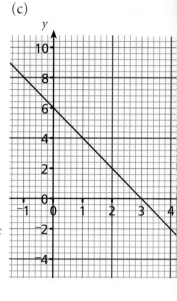

7 (a) What is the gradient of the line with equation $y = 12x - 20$?

(b) What is the y-intercept for the line?

8 Write down the gradient and y-intercept of each of these lines

(a) $y = x + 7$ (b) $y = 5 - 4x.$ (c) $y = {}^-6x - 1$

9 This diagram shows two lines, P and Q.

(a) Write down the equation of line P.

(b) Write down the equation of any other line that is parallel to P.

(c) Write down the equation of line Q.

(d) Write down the equation of any other line that is parallel to Q.

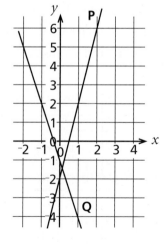

10 What is the equation of the line parallel to $y = 1.5x - 3$ that crosses the y-axis at $(0, 7)$?

11 Write down the equation of the line with y-intercept 5 that is parallel to $y = 3 - 9x$.

12 The lines labelled A to D match these equations.

$y = 2x - 4$

$y = 2x + 4$

$y = x - 4$

$y = {}^-2x + 4$

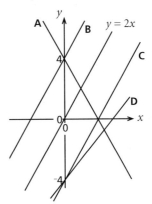

Match each line to its correct equation.

You will need to draw suitable axes for each of the next three questions.

13 (a) Draw the line that passes through point (2, 1) and has gradient 2.

(b) Write down the equation of the line.

14 (a) Write down the gradient and y-intercept of the line $y = 3x + 4$.

(b) Draw this line.

15 Draw the line with equation $y = 2x - 5$.

Section C

1 For each of the lines A to F

(a) find the gradient as a fraction.

(b) find the y-intercept.

(c) write down its equation.

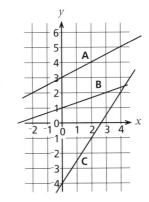

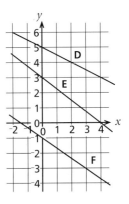

2 Which of these lines is steeper: $y = \frac{1}{2}x + 3$ or $y = \frac{1}{3}x - 1$?

3 What is the equation of the line that passes through $({}^-5, 0)$ and $(0, 2)$?

4 The lines labelled P, Q R and S match these equations.

$y = \frac{1}{2}x + 3$

$y = \frac{3}{2}x + 3$

$y = {}^-\frac{1}{2}x + 3$

$y = \frac{4}{5}x + 3$

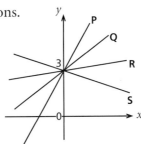

Match each line to its correct equation.

5 (a) Match the equations below to give three pairs of parallel lines.

A $y = \frac{2}{3}x + 3$ **B** $y = 4 - \frac{1}{5}x + 3$ **C** $y = 2 + \frac{1}{4}x$ **D** $y = 2 - \frac{x}{4}$

E $y = \frac{x}{4} - 2$ **F** $y = \frac{2}{3}x - 5$ **G** $y = {}^-2 - \frac{x}{5}$

(b) Which one is the odd one out?

Section D

1 Find the gradient of each of these lines.

(a) $y - x = 4$ (b) $y - 2x = 3$ (c) $x + y = 7$

(d) $4x = y - 2$ (e) $5x + y = 2$ (f) $y + 10 = 3x$

2 Match the equations below to give three pairs of parallel lines.

A $y - 2x = 7$ **B** $y + x = 5$ **C** $2x = y - 4$

D $y + 2x = 15$ **E** $y = 3 - 2x$ **F** $y = 8 - x$

3 Find the gradients of each of these lines.

(a) $3y = 9x - 6$ (b) $2y = 4 - 6x$ (c) $4y - 12x = 8$ (d) $2y + 9x = 4$

4 Find the gradients and y-intercepts of each of these lines.

(a) $2y = x$ (b) $5y = x - 10$ (c) $4y = 2x + 3$

5 The lines labelled G, H, I and J match these equations.

$x + y = 2$ $y - x = 2$

$y - 5x = 2$ $2y - x = 4$

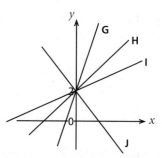

Match each line to its correct equation.

6 Which two of the following lines are

(a) parallel to the line $y = 3x - 1$

(b) parallel to the line $y = \frac{1}{3}x + 1$

A $3x = y + 2$ **B** $3y = x - 2$

C $x + 3y = 1$ **D** $x - 3y = 5$

E $y + 3x = 2$ **F** $3x - y = 3$

*7 Find an equation for the line parallel to $2y - x = 8$ that has y-intercept 5.

Section E

1 A small ball was thrown vertically downwards from the top of a high building and its speed was measured at various times during its fall.

The results were plotted and the line of best fit drawn.

(a) Find the gradient of the line of best fit.

(b) Find the vertical intercept.

(c) Write down an approximate equation for the line of best fit.

(d) Use your equation to estimate the speed of the ball after 5 seconds.

(e) What was the initial speed with which the ball was thrown?

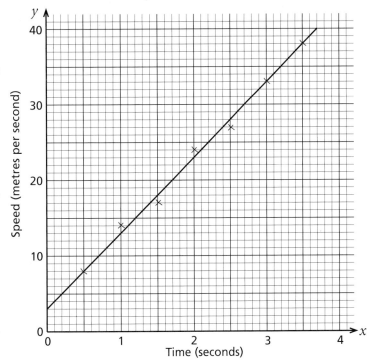

2 A ball is dropped from various different heights and the height to which it bounces is recorded.

This graph shows the results and a line of best fit has been drawn.

(a) Find the gradient of the line of best fit.

(b) What is the vertical intercept?

(c) Write down an approximate equation for the line of best fit.

(d) Use your equation to estimate the height of the rebound if the ball is dropped from a height of 4 metres.

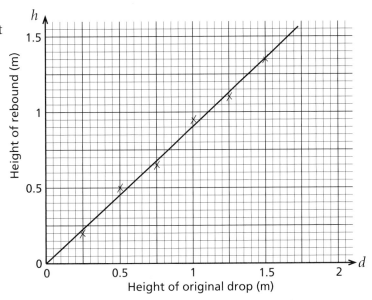

Mixed questions 6

1 Work out the value of $3^n - 1$ when
  (a) $n = 2$ (b) $n = 4$ (c) $n = 1$ (d) $n = {}^-1$

2 Expand these.
  (a) $7(p - q)$ (b) $4(a + 3c)$ (c) $p(p - 3q)$ (d) $5xy(3x - 4)$

3 (a) The straight line p joins the point $(4, 2)$ to point $(10, 7)$.
      What is the gradient of p?
  (b) What is the distance between the two points, to one decimal place?
  (c) Sort these straight lines into gradient order, starting with the least steep.
        q $(1, 3)$ to $(10, 6)$ r $(3, 1)$ to $(12, 3)$ s $(2, 2)$ to $(9, 4)$ t $({}^-2, 4)$ to $(2, 5)$
  (d) What is the distance between each pair of points in (c), to one d.p.?

4 Factorise these expressions completely.
  (a) $5x^2 - 5xy$ (b) $8ab^2 + 2$ (c) $9y^3 - 12x^2y$ (d) $6p^2q + 10pq^2$

5 Find the equation of this
  straight line graph.

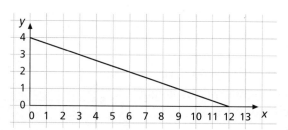

6 Solve these equations
  (a) $3^x = 243$ (b) $x^5 = 32$ (c) $9^x = 1$ (d) $x^{-2} = 0.04$

7 Write the area of the shaded square
  as simply as possible in terms of x.

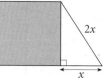

8 Write the answers to these using indices.
  (a) $8^{10} \div 8^2$ (b) $9^5 \times 9^3$ (c) $\dfrac{4^5 \times 4^4}{4^3}$ (d) $\dfrac{3^9}{3^3 \times 3^5}$

9 This is a regular nonagon (nine-sided polygon)
  with two diagonals drawn.

  Calculate the angles marked with letters.

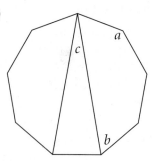